Ichiro Suzuki

By Jeff Savage

AMAZING
ATHLETES

LERNERSPORTS / Minneapolis

This book is available in two editions:
Library binding by LernerSports
Soft cover by First Avenue Editions
Imprints of Lerner Publishing Group
241 First Avenue North
Minneapolis, MN 55401 U.S.A.

Website address: www.lernerbooks.com

Library of Congress Cataloging-in-Publication Data

Savage, Jeff, 1961–
      Ichiro Suzuki / by Jeff Savage.
         p.   cm. — (Amazing athletes)
      Includes index.
      Summary: Introduces the life and accomplishments of champion baseball player Ichiro Suzuki, the first Japanese position player to switch from the Japanese League to the Major Leagues.
      ISBN: 0-8225-1344-7 (lib. bdg. : alk. paper)
      ISBN: 0-8225-3687-0 (pbk. : alk. paper)
      1. Suzuki, Ichiráo, 1973– — Juvenile literature. 2. Baseball players—Japan—Biography—Juvenile literature. [1. Suzuki, Ichiráo, 1973– 2. Baseball players.] I. Title. II. Series.
GV865.S895 S38   2003
796.357'092—dc21   2002151700

Manufactured in the United States of America
1 2 3 4 5 6 – DP – 08 07 06 05 04 03

TABLE OF CONTENTS

Before Ichiro goes to bat, he stretches his body. He even exercises while he's in right field.

A FAST START

Ichiro Suzuki, a native of Japan, came to the plate to bat for the Seattle Mariners at the team's home field. Before stepping into the **batter's box,** though, he did an exercise. He slowly bent over at the waist. His face nearly touched the ground. Ichiro does this motion to find balance.

The sellout crowd of 45,000 people watched Ichiro's ritual. In Japan, millions more watched on television. They had seen the motion before. He had just joined the Mariners at right field to become the first Japanese non-pitcher to enter Major League Baseball.

Japanese American fans show their support for Ichiro.

Ichiro is Japan's all-time batting champ. American fans looked forward to seeing his powerful skill.

Ichiro is quick! He can run from home plate to first base in 3.7 seconds.

More than 100 newspaper and TV reporters from Japan were in Seattle to see Ichiro's first game. They knew what Ichiro could do. Baseball fans in America were about to find out.

Ichiro made outs his first three times at bat. But in the seventh inning, Ichiro smashed a ball that whistled past the pitcher and into center field for a **single.** The Mariners were trailing the Oakland A's by one run, but not for long. On the next hit, Ichiro raced around the bases to score. The game was tied, 4–4.

After making a few outs, Ichiro got on base in the team's season opener against the Oakland A's.

Seattle fans have a lot to cheer about with Ichiro on their home team.

In the eighth inning, Carlos Guillen stood on first base when Ichiro came to bat once more. "EE-chee-ro! EE-chee-ro!" the fans chanted.

Ichiro responded by smartly **bunting** the ball down the **first-base line.** He blazed to first base so fast that the A's pitcher panicked and threw the ball away. Guillen eventually scored the winning run. The crowd cheered for Ichiro. He smiled and waved. Later, he told reporters, "The feelings I have tonight I will never forget."

Ichiro's bunt in the eighth inning helped the Mariners win their first game of the season.

Ichiro, like kids all over Japan, joined his local Little League team to improve his baseball skills.

LEARNING THE GAME

Ichiro Suzuki was born October 22, 1973, in Kasugai, Japan. His first name is pronounced "ee-chee-ro." It means "first boy." Some say it also translates to "fast man."

Baseball is a popular sport in Japan, just as it is in America. Ichiro grew up in Nagoya and began playing with a baseball at age three. He rode his bicycle to elementary school and earned good grades. By second grade, he had completely fallen in love with baseball. He wanted to become a great player someday.

Japan, Ichiro's home country, is long and narrow. His hometown of Nagoya is a big port city in central Japan where cloth, bicycles, and other products are made.

11

Ichiro joined his hometown Little League team. His father, Nobuyuki, became coach of the team. The team played only on Sundays. Ichiro knew he would need to play more than once a week to become great. So he and his father practiced every day after school. Ichiro worked hard on fundamentals such as bunting, hitting, and baserunning.

An American schoolteacher introduced baseball to Japan in the 1870s. By the 1930s, the first professional Japanese leagues were in place. By the 1970s, when Ichiro started to become interested in baseball, the sport was well established.

Ichiro went to Aiko-Dai Meiden High School in Nagoya. He was a star on the school's baseball team. Twice he played in Koshien, the national high school baseball tournament in

Japan. He impressed Japanese professional **scouts.** Upon his graduation from high school, he was **drafted** by a team called the Orix Blue Wave as their right fielder.

Ichiro pitched during Koshien, the Japanese national high school baseball tournament.

Kobe, home of the Orix Blue Wave, is a huge city in central Japan. Ichiro still lives there in the off-season.

TURNING PRO

Ichiro had achieved his dream. He had become a pro baseball player. The Blue Wave played their home games in Kobe, a port city of nearly two million people. But before Ichiro could join the Blue Wave, he played in the **minor leagues.** There he learned how to hit pro pitching and perfected his sprint around the bases.

In 1993, Ichiro was called up to the Blue Wave. He quickly became a star in Japan. In Ichiro's first full season, he set a record with 210 hits. He led the league in batting average and was named the 1994 Japanese Pacific League's Most Valuable Player (MVP).

Ichiro improved his blinding speed around the bases in the minor leagues.

The next year, he led in batting average again. He also ranked first in runs batted in (RBI) and **stolen bases.** He was named league MVP again. In 1996, he led the Blue Wave to the Japan Series championship. He was an easy choice as league MVP again.

With the Orix Blue
Wave, Ichiro became
an outstanding batter.
He won the Japanese
Pacific League's
batting award seven
times in a row.

Ichiro's style stood out in many ways. He threw from right field with his right hand, yet he batted left-handed.

In the batter's box, he aimed his bat toward the pitcher. He looked as if he was about to duel with a sword. He swung with quick wrists and a slashing swing.

Ichiro was equally skilled in the outfield of the Blue Wave team. Here, he slides to make a catch.

Ichiro followed up his hits with incredible running speed. He not only reached first base quickly but was often able to steal additional bases.

Upon making contact, Ichiro put on a burst of speed to reach first base. And in the outfield, Ichiro's ability to chase down balls was matched by his powerful throwing arm.

Ichiro had become the most popular baseball player in Japan. The team's souvenir shops sold Ichiro cups, key chains, baseballs, jerseys, T-shirts, posters, stickers, notebooks, pins, and flags. He was known throughout Japan simply as Ichiro. His coach even changed the name on the back of his uniform from Suzuki to Ichiro.

In a game against a team from Osaka, Japan, Ichiro made an incredible catch to save the game.

Ichiro thanked his many Japanese fans at his last game as a Blue Wave. He had decided to join the American major leagues.

AN INSTANT HIT

In 2000, Ichiro won the Japanese batting title for the seventh straight time. He had become so famous that a letter addressed simply to "Ichiro, Japan" would reach his mailbox. A poll named him the most recognizable person in Japan, just ahead of the emperor of Japan.

But Ichiro wanted to play baseball in North America, where baseball had begun. Many major league baseball teams wanted him. The Seattle Mariners offered the most money. They paid $13 million to the Blue Wave and $15 million to Ichiro. Ichiro was sad to leave Japan but excited to come to America. "I go, but another star soon will replace me," Ichiro said.

Ichiro was all smiles after signing his contract to play for the Seattle Mariners in December of 2000.

Ichiro meets the press after a workout with the Mariners in Seattle in January 2001.

When Ichiro joined the Mariners for the 2001 season, seven Japanese pitchers were on major league rosters. However, Ichiro became the first non-pitcher to join Major League Baseball. Some predicted that Ichiro would do well. Others thought he would be a bust. "Sometimes I am nervous, sometimes anxious," said Ichiro. "But I want to challenge a new world."

Ichiro was an instant hit. He had his first great game on Opening Day. A few days later, he hit a game-winning **home run** in extra innings. The next day, he made a laserlike throw from right field to nail a base runner at third base.

Seattle fans got used to seeing Ichiro's incredible catches and throws from right field.

Ichiro faced a fellow Japanese player, Shigetoshi Hasegawa *(above)* of the Anaheim Angels, during his first season. Hasegawa later joined Ichiro on the Mariners team.

Two nights later, in a game against the Anaheim Angels, he singled off Shigetoshi Hasegawa. Hasegawa had been Ichiro's former teammate with the Orix Blue Wave. This was the first time an Asian batter faced an Asian pitcher in the major leagues. After Ichiro's single, the baseball was boxed up and sent to the National Baseball Hall of Fame.

The Mariners won 116 games to tie the major league record for most victories in one season. Ichiro hit .350 to win the league batting title. He also led the league in hits and stolen bases.

A player's batting average is arrived at by dividing the number of hits a player has by the number of times the player was at bat.

Stealing bases is another of Ichiro's strengths. He led the league in stolen bases in his rookie American year.

In the playoffs, he batted a record .600 to lead the Mariners past the Cleveland Indians in five games. Seattle was one step from reaching the World Series for the first time in its twenty-five-year history. But its magical season ended against the New York Yankees.

In 2001, Seattle reached the American League Championship. Here, Ichiro makes a sliding catch during a game against the New York Yankees. The Yankees eventually ended Seattle's 2001 season.

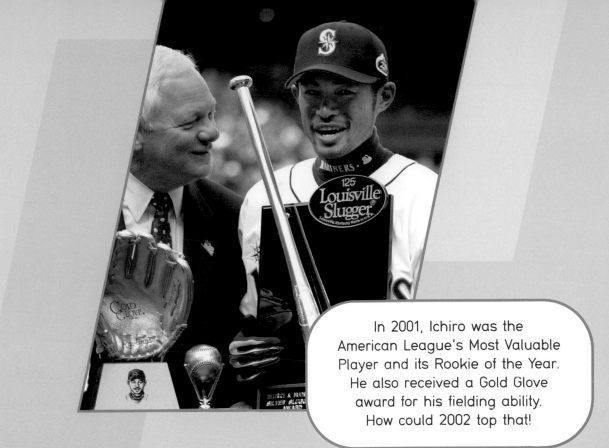

In 2001, Ichiro was the American League's Most Valuable Player and its Rookie of the Year. He also received a Gold Glove award for his fielding ability. How could 2002 top that!

THE WIZARD

Ichiro came out even hotter in 2002. He hit safely in thirty of his first thirty-three games, reaching base every way possible. In one game, he bunted for a base hit *twice*. In another, he slapped hits down the left-field line and right-field line *twice each*.

Fans have become used to seeing Ichiro in his stylish sunglasses. He wears them to protect his vision.

The Mariners raced out front for the playoffs, with Ichiro leading the way. He grew skinny sideburns and wore cool sunglasses. His teammates called him the Wizard.

He received more fan votes for the All-Star Game than any other player. The most popular food item at Seattle's Safeco Field was the Ichi Roll from the sushi stand. At souvenir shops, fans were paying $500 for his autograph on a baseball.

Everyone wanted to know more about Ichiro. He didn't say much, though, and even declined to give out the name of his dog.

The Mariners, A's, and Angels battled to make the playoffs. Ichiro did all he could to lead his team. For the 2002 season, he finished fourth in the league in batting, with a .321 average. Unfortunately, the Mariners missed the playoffs.

But there will be more chances with Ichiro leading the way. He has become a national hero in *two* countries.

Ichiro likes to play golf. He is able to play often in the United States. That isn't the case when he's in Japan. "I can't play in Japan because every golf course has caddies," Ichiro explained. "The caddies all want autographs and don't want to let me play golf."

Selected Career Highlights

2002 won his second Gold Glove award
finished second in hits in American League
led Majors in All-Star ballotting for second year

2001 won American League batting title
won his first American Gold Glove award
led the American League in stolen bases
named American League's Most Valuable Player
named American League's Rookie of the Year
led Majors in All-Star ballotting

2000 won seventh straight Japanese Pacific League batting title

1999 won sixth straight Japanese Pacific League batting title

1998 won fifth straight Japanese Pacific League batting title

1997 won fourth straight Japanese Pacific League batting title

1996 named Japanese Pacific League's Most Valuable Player
won third straight Japanese Pacific League batting title

1995 named Japanese Pacific League's Most Valuable Player
won second straight Japanese Pacific League batting title

1994 named Japanese Pacific League's Most Valuable Player
won Japanese Pacific League batting title

Glossary

batter's box: the rectangular area next to home plate in which the batter stands

bunt: a short hit that doesn't involve swinging the bat. Bunting surprises the opposing players and advances a teammate already on base.

draft: a yearly event in which all professional teams in a major league sport are given the chance to pick new players from a selected group. Most of the players in the group have played their sport in college.

first-base line: the white chalk line that extends from home plate to first base. Inside the line, a batted ball is fair or in play. Outside the line, a batted ball is foul and not in play.

home run: a play in which the batter hits the ball and circles the bases safely to cross home plate

minor leagues: the lower leagues where young players improve their playing skills. It is one step below the major leagues.

professional: a person who is paid money to play

scout: a person who reviews the playing skills of young players

single: a play in which the batter hits the ball and safely reaches first base

stolen base: an act in which a runner on base advances to the next base without aid

Further Reading & Websites

Rains, Rob. *Baseball Samurais: Ichiro Suzuki and the Asian Invasion.* New York: St. Martin's Paperbacks, 2001.

Shields, David. *Baseball Is Just Baseball: The Understated Ichiro.* Seattle, WA: TNI Books, 2001.

Stewart, Mark. *Ichiro Suzuki: Best in the West.* Brookfield, CT: The Millbrook Press, 2002.

Collectibles Website
<http://www.ichirocollectables.com>
A fan website that has Ichiro memorabilia such as posters, pennants, and autographed baseballs.

Ichiro Trading Cards
<http://www.ichirorookies.com>
A website that tells all about Ichiro's trading cards.

Official MLB Site
<http://www.mlb.com>
The official Major League Baseball website that provides fans with game action, biographies of players, and information about baseball.

Sports Illustrated for Kids
<http://www.sikids.com>
The *Sports Illustrated for Kids* website that covers all sports, including baseball.

Index

Photo Acknowledgments

Photographs are used with the permission of: © Michael Zito/SportsChrome, pp. 4, 23; © AFP/CORBIS, pp. 7, 22, 27; © Reuters NewMedia, Inc./CORBIS, pp. 5, 6, 30; © Natalie Fobes/CORBIS, p. 8; © Otto Greule Jr./Getty Images, p. 9, 26; © Robert Holmes/CORBIS, p. 10; © Steve Kaufman/CORBIS, p. 11; © Kyodo News Agency, pp. 13, 16, 17, 18, 19, 20, 21; © Michael S. Yamashita/CORBIS, p. 14; © Jeff Gross/Getty Images, p. 24; © Rob Tringali Jr./SportsChrome, p. 25; © Duomo/CORBIS, p. 28.

Cover: © Otto Greule Jr./Getty Images.